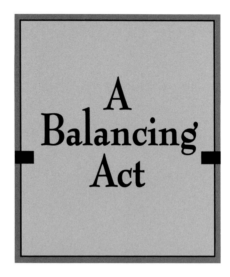

A
Balancing
Act

A Balancing Act

SPORTS
— and —
EDUCATION

GARY FUNK

Lerner Publications Company ■ Minneapolis

rents

*The Publisher thanks Jay Coakley, Ph.D., Professor of
Sociology at the University of Colorado, Colorado Springs,
Colorado, for his assistance.*

Library of Congress Cataloging-in-Publication Data

Funk, Gary D., 1958–
    A balancing act : sports and education / by Gary Funk.
        p. cm. — (Sports issues)
    Includes bibliographical references and index.
    ISBN 0–8225–3301–4
    1. School sports—United States—Juvenile literature. 2. College
athletes—Education—United States—Juvenile literature. 3. High
school athletes—Education—United States—Juvenile literature.
4. School sports—Corrupt practices—United States—Juvenile
literature. [1. School sports. 2. Athletes.] I. Title.
    II. Series.
GV346.F85   1995
796.04'2—dc20   94–38597
                                                                      CIP
                                                                        AC

Manufactured in the United States of America

1 2 3 4 5 6 – I/JR – 00 99 98 97 96 95

CONTENTS

CHAPTER ONE

BALANCING THE BALL: ATHLETICS AND ACADEMICS

■

American sports are full of wonderful images. A basketball player soars over defenders for a graceful dunk. Entire towns celebrate high school state championships. Olympic champions achieve their dreams. These are the beautiful portraits of sports—a world where determination, practice, and competition blend together in exhilarating fashion.

Sports has an ugly side, too. Fistfights often dominate televised highlights of National Hockey League games. Two Chicagoans die in 1993 during riotous "celebrations" after the Chicago Bulls win their third consecutive National Basketball Association (NBA) title. A youth league baseball parent in Springfield, Missouri, is escorted off the field after punching an umpire. For these players and fans, sportsmanship evidently means little.

The relationship between sports and education mirrors these various images of sports. The conflicts between academics and athletics have been the subject of much debate. Do colleges take advantage of young student-athletes by selling their athletic skills to the sports-loving public? Or do

Rex Walters led his University of Kansas men's basketball team in the NCAA Final Four tournament before graduating with honors.

student-athletes cheat themselves out of an education by focusing on their fastballs instead of their physics? Who's responsible for making sure student-athletes are students as well as athletes?

Duke University's graduation rate for men's basketball players since 1986 is 100 percent. Compare that to the 0 percent graduation rate for male athletes at the University of Alabama.[1] The sportsmanship of successful Baltimore DeMatha High School coach Morgan Wooten seems noble when compared to the actions of University of Arkansas at Pine Bluff football coach, Archie "The Gunslinger" Cooley, whose 1990 team included assistant coaches and ineligible players using assumed names.

Rex Walters, star guard for the University of Kansas's 1993 Final Four team, capped off his senior year by graduating with honors and doing NCAA public service announcements on the importance of education. Allen Iverson, Virginia's 1992–93 High School Player of the Year in football and basketball, began his senior season awaiting sentencing for three felony convictions stemming from a violent brawl.[2] With such a wide range of actions and behaviors, the relationship between sports and education can be confusing.

Are athletics emphasized too much in American schools? Or does a proper balance exist? Do students benefit from playing sports? Or does their schoolwork suffer? Do high schools and universities profit from winning teams? Or are vast amounts of money wasted? Are there reasonable solutions to the many problems facing athletics in our schools? Or is the situation beyond reform? These are difficult questions. Only a careful examination of the relationship between sports and education will provide meaningful answers.

JUSTIFYING SPORTS

Athletic competition has long been glorified for its character-building values. Beginning with the first Greek Olympic Games in 776 B.C., the Games had an almost religious quality for the athletes and spectators. The Greek writer Lucian (c. A.D. 120–200) explained the importance of early Greek Olympics when he told a visitor, ". . . telling you how delightful the Games are will not really convince you. You should sit there yourself, among the spectators, and see the

Greeks in ancient times glorified athletic competition and created many statues, vases, and other artworks depicting sports activities. This statue shows a discus thrower.

fine contestants, how beautiful and healthy their bodies are, their marvelous skill and unbeatable strength, their daring and ambition, their firm resolve and their absolute will to win."[3] Lucian's reflections on the wonders of sports still reflect the feelings of some people in the present day.

Those who like athletics cite a number of benefits derived from

Auburn University's football team in 1893 used considerably less equipment than football teams in 1993 did.

participating in sports. Doctors have long advised that a healthy body promotes a healthy mind. Studies of brain development and function show that physical activity stimulates brain cell development.[4] Advocates of sports speak of how sports participation builds character. Athletes develop determination, according to these advocates. Through practice and competition, athletes understand the importance of self-sacrifice, teamwork, self-discipline, and concentration.

As early as 1893, Massachusetts Institute of Technology president Francis A. Walker maintained that to play football an athlete must have "courage, coolness, steadiness of nerve, quickness of apprehension, resourcefulness, self-knowl-

edge, self-reliance." Walker said it promoted "something akin to patriotism and public spirit."[5]

Even those who award the famous Rhodes scholarship agree that sports participation can benefit scholars. The Rhodes scholarship, which was established by British businessman Cecil J. Rhodes, pays for scholars from around the world to attend England's Oxford University. The academic requirements for receiving a Rhodes scholarship are high, but candidates must also display "personal vigor," which is generally accepted as athletic ability. Senator Bill Bradley, one-time basketball star at Princeton University and with the New York Knicks of the NBA, is one of the most famous Rhodes scholars. Nnenna Lynch, the national 3,000-meter college track champion in 1992, maintained an A-average throughout her college career at Villanova and was named a Rhodes scholar.[6]

LINKING SCHOOLS AND SPORTS

American schools have not always sponsored athletic competition. No intercollegiate sporting events were held until 1852, when the rowing teams from Harvard University and Yale University raced. Amherst College and Williams College squared off in baseball in 1859, and the first college football contest in 1869 featured squads from Rutgers University and Princeton University. These early college sporting events lacked the support of faculties and school officials, but their popularity with students and alumni increased with each passing year.[7] It wasn't

These students played intercollegiate baseball for Rutgers University in 1890.

long before intercollegiate athletic competition became a familiar part of the college scene.

High school sports were quick to follow, and the first decade of the twentieth century saw an explosion of high school and college competition. By the beginning of World War I, football, basketball, track, and baseball were common activities for male students in high schools and colleges. Opportunities for female students were fewer, but several states sponsored basketball and track for high school girls. Towns competed against rival towns, teams vied for state championships, and spirited loyalties grew. Sports participation became widespread, and the athletic battles for glory drew more and more attention from fans and journalists.

Sports competition in the United States also became very "American" for men. Sports came to be viewed similarly to serving in the military. Competition on the playing field has often been compared to combat on the battlefield. Most sporting events begin with the national anthem. The anthem is rarely played before plays, musical performances, or even something as important as high school or college graduation ceremonies.

America is not the only nation to view sports, war, and patriotism together. National pride and athletic accomplishment seem to go hand in hand around the world. World Cup soccer games incite passions in fans from Sweden to Colombia.

WIN ONE FOR THE GIPPER

The attention given to athletics wasn't always positive. As organized sports flourished at the turn of the century, educators, politicians, and journalists began debating the value of school-sponsored athletic competition. President Theodore Roosevelt openly criticized excesses in college sports, and the *New York Times* compared football to the evils of lynching. By 1934 more than 40 studies had examined the academic progress of high school

and college athletes. The recommendations of these studies were mixed, but a warning had been sounded.[9]

School sports also had defenders—including legendary University of Notre Dame football coach Knute Rockne. Responding to those who questioned the worth of high school and college football, Rockne quipped that youngsters should be given "footballs instead of guns."[10]

It was Rockne himself who would give the sporting public a taste of things to come. Star Notre Dame halfback George Gipp was

Knute Rockne

George Gipp was an All-American halfback for Notre Dame in 1919, but his academic performance didn't match his athletic prowess. Gipp wouldn't be eligible to play for the Fighting Irish in the 1990s.

expelled for poor grades in 1919. After local citizens petitioned the university president, Gipp was allowed to reenter school and play football. Coach Rockne justified this surprising twist by claiming Gipp had "amazed" school officials with his answers to a set of oral examinations.[11]

Rockne also took the "spirit of combat" idea a step further. The popular 1940 movie, *Knute Rockne, All American,* provides a glimpse of Rockne's ultimate vision of the potential of college football. In the movie, Rockne says competitive games could be a substitute for war and revolution. Football coaches, claimed Rockne, believe "the finest work of man is building the character of man." Rockne's biographer, Michael R. Steele, wrote that Rockne even believed football could be "used to promote international understanding and harmony."[12]

CALLING THE SHOTS

The National Collegiate Athletic Association (NCAA) and the National Federation of State High School Associations (NFSHSA) were formed to promote the positive values of sports. The NCAA was founded in 1905 as the Inter-national Athletic Association of the United States. In 1910 the organization changed its name to the current NCAA. The NCAA's purpose has always been to provide intercollegiate athletics with standard rules.

College students complained about the NCAA from the beginning. They were upset because the organization's rules ended the freedom students had enjoyed in running their own athletic contests. But the 18 deaths and 149 serious injuries during the 1905 college football season prompted school administrators and influential alumni to take over the organization of school sports.[13]

For several years the NCAA was solely a "discussion group and rules-making body."[14] In 1921, however, the NCAA held its first national championships in track and field. As the popularity of college sports (particularly men's basketball and football) grew, the organization made rules for recruiting, financial aid, and academic standards.

The National Federation of State High School Associations began in Chicago, Illinois, on May 14, 1920. Its original purpose was to control the high school activities being organized by colleges and promoters.[15] Less centralized than the NCAA, the NFSHSA is now made up of 50 state high school athletic associations. Although the state organizations are independent and have their own rules, they adhere to the same basic principles.

Besides regulating their members' activities, the NCAA and NFSHSA are committed to promoting the ideals of sport. Both claim to promote a healthy balance between athletics and academics. Is this the case, though? Current expectations of student-athletes suggest the "athlete" may receive more attention and acclaim than the "student" does.

Solutions to the problems revolving around sports and education in the modern era are not as simple as they were in 1919. Coach Rockne's explanation of

GOALS OF SCHOOL SPORTS

From the Missouri State High School Activities Association 1993–94 Official Handbook:

"Interscholastic activities shall supplement the secondary curricular program and shall provide most worthwhile experiences to students that shall result in those learning outcomes that will contribute toward the development of the attributes of good citizenship. Emphasis shall be upon teaching 'through' school activities. To this end only can interscholastic activities be justified."

The NCAA's mission statement:
- To initiate, stimulate, and improve intercollegiate athletics programs for student-athletes.
- To encourage members to comply with satisfactory standards of scholarship, sportsmanship, and amateurism.
- To set rules of play for intercollegiate sports.
- To preserve intercollegiate athletics records.
- To establish eligibility standards for regional and national athletic events.
- To establish standards so colleges and universities can maintain their athletics programs on a high level.

Gipp's oral examinations wouldn't be accepted by today's investigative journalists or the public. In fact, the relationship between academics and athletics is often criticized and questioned.

Books such as Rick Telander's *The Hundred Yard Lie* and Richard E. Lapchick's *On The Mark* have examined the ethics of athletic competition. The NCAA Presidents' Commission (1988), the Women's Sports Foundation (1989), and even *USA Today* (1993) are among the many organizations that have studied how playing sports affects students' academic success. Even the U.S. legislature has been involved, as both the House of Representatives and the Senate have debated laws about college athletics.

CHAPTER TWO

ALL THINGS
TO ALL PEOPLE

■

Student-athletes are expected to do well in a number of areas. They are expected to be good students. They are expected to be outstanding citizens. They are expected to win. Mack Brown, University of North Carolina football coach, addressed his team before a big game with Florida State in 1993 as a national television audience watched. During the pregame pep talk, Coach Brown reminded his players of his recruiting promise that they would "play big-time football, graduate from a great university, and have a chance to be in the Top Ten." Although

North Carolina lost the game 33–7, the message in Coach Brown's pep talk was admirable.

Unfortunately, competing, winning, and graduating aren't as simple as listening to a pep talk. Many high school and college student-athletes can achieve these goals, but the task is more difficult for others. And their task is even tougher when the message about winning comes across louder than the message about grades.

Every small American town boasts billboards advertising local restaurants and motels, a listing of churches in the community,

and a city limits sign. In many locales, the biggest and brightest signs honor the accomplishments of local sports heroes. "The Birthplace of Jim Thorpe" says a freshly painted sign outside of Yale, Oklahoma. "Home of the 1990 State AA High School Baseball Champions" proclaims a huge sign along a highway entering Billings, Missouri. Example after example of publicity for athletic success in America's towns and cities can be given. How often, though, have signs been erected for students receiving National Merit Finalist designation? How often have communities bragged to visitors about former high school students who have graduated with honors from top colleges?

Newspapers sometimes print articles on education, but they devote an entire daily section to sports! Television news mirrors newspapers, and weekend TV viewers are bombarded with an endless array of games. University of Minnesota researchers analyzed Minneapolis–St. Paul television stations and discovered one station that devoted 30 minutes to high school athletics for every one minute spent covering high school academic and artistic accomplishments. In fact, the study found that only one Minneapolis–St. Paul television station spent more time covering high school academics than athletics.[1] Academic achievements do not seem as newsworthy as victories on the football field or the basketball court.

WINNING IS EVERYTHING, ISN'T IT?

Other events also raise questions about the balance between athletics and academics. In Republic, Missouri, boys' basketball coach Denny Hunt was fired in 1991. Hunt, whose record at Republic High School was 84–25, was considered to be a good teacher who demanded discipline and sportsmanship from his players. Hunt was doomed, though, after his team lost in consecutive seasons to nearby Clever, Missouri, a smaller school with an enrollment of barely 100. These defeats were humiliating to some school board members, who promptly fired Hunt without giving a reason and hired the coach from the victorious Clever team. In 1993 the Lebanon, Indiana, high school boys' basketball coach was fired.

The coach had won 64 percent of his games and captured four sectional titles during his five years as coach. The Lebanon school board blamed the firing on declining fan attendance.[2]

Don Donoher had been the men's basketball coach at the University of Dayton for more than two decades. His overall record was 437–275, and he was the most successful coach in University of Dayton history. He was widely respected for his sportsmanship and commitment to student-athletes. In 1989, however, Donoher's squad recorded a losing season, and his team did not make the NCAA postseason tournament. Losing out on the hundreds of thousands of dollars awarded to NCAA tourney teams was more than Dayton officials could bear, and Donoher was forced to resign.

Eddie Sutton, head basketball coach at Oklahoma State University, and Jackie Sherrill, head football coach at Mississippi State University, represent the same stress on winning but from a different point of view. Sutton was forced to resign from the University of Kentucky because of scandals about athletes' grades. He was hired for the Oklahoma State position because of his ability to win games. Sherrill, forced to resign from Texas A&M because of major NCAA violations, was quickly hired at Mississippi State University because of his success on the field. Coaches who lose jobs due to wrongdoing are quickly hired by other schools if they have shown they can produce victories.

What signals do these actions send to student-athletes? When successful coaches are fired after one bad season or one embarrassing loss, a "must-win" attitude is communicated to players and fans alike. Winning itself may not even be enough for some people.

For these people, who you beat may be even more important.

Student-athletes pick up on these obvious messages. Compare how many teachers have been fired because their students didn't get high test scores versus the number of coaches who have been fired for losing seasons. Poor teaching in math, science, or social studies can be tolerated, but losing too many athletic contests cannot. The values of many communities and school boards can be seen through these actions. Hundreds or thousands of people showing up at an athletic event is

a powerful message in itself. Students know how seldom people visit their classes or go to see a debate tournament.

BEAT THE CLOCK

Along with the mixed signals about what's important, the time demands of playing sports and studying make achieving both goals difficult. High school practices in any varsity sport will demand as much as 20 hours a week in meetings, practice, games, and travel. This is more time than most high school students spend studying. A U.S. Department of Education study found that 68 percent of American high school seniors studied fewer than five hours a week. This same study reported that 70 percent of high school seniors said poor study habits interfered with getting good grades. These statistics were supported by the findings of a large midwestern university where 76 percent of the freshmen students admitted to studying fewer than five hours per week. In fact, the freshmen at this institution on average had studied for barely more than four hours a week in high school.[3]

Even if high school student-

athletes wanted to spend more time studying, it would be difficult. Most high schools are in session seven hours a day. Practices can take up to three hours daily. Of course, everybody must eat and sleep, so little time is left for

anything else, let alone something as arduous as studying. Music, drama, and other extracurricular activities demand time as well. But these activities rarely involve the number of weekends, evenings, and trips that go along with varsity athletics.

The time demands of high school athletics are mild when compared to those of college sports. With more intense practicing and a greater emphasis on weight training and team meetings, college athletics take up 30 or more hours a week. A 1988 National Study of Intercollegiate Athletics found most college students —athletes in particular—were more concerned with time demands than any other topic. The study reported that:

• Student-athletes spent more time in their sports than nonathletes did in their recreational activities.
• College football and basketball players spent nearly 30 hours per week in their sports while they were in season—more time than the combined time they spent preparing for and attending class.
• In season, student-athletes missed about two classes per week, while nonathletes missed about one class per week.
• Freshman student-athletes spent as much time in their sports as older student-athletes.

A sophomore women's basketball player was quoted in the report: "It's much harder being a student-athlete. I don't have time for myself. I feel owned and I feel like I always have to be here or there. My grades dropped due to this. My coach doesn't remember that we have homework. She says academics is first, but it's not true."[4]

Travel to and from games adds to the problem. College student-athletes often miss days of classes when traveling for road games. A study by a college Geography of Sport class discovered some college basketball teams travel as many as 40,000 miles a year to play games. This amounts to 81 hours of air travel—roughly two full work weeks![5] This is an extreme example, but many college teams routinely rack up thousands of travel miles a year.

A 1989 NCAA report included the comments of anonymous student-athletes from across the nation. A sophomore football player voiced the frustrations of some student-athletes: "I believe that

Jamelle Holieway hit the books, along with the weights, while attending the University of Oklahoma. He played quarterback for the Sooners. A knee injury ended his football career and allegations of wrongdoing tainted his reputation.

being a football player takes up too much time. People may say, 'You're a student first,' but actually they control each week of your life with few exceptions."[6]

In the early 1990s, the NCAA began taking steps to ease the time demands on student-athletes. The practice season was shortened, the number of games was limited, and other reforms were implemented.[7] Still, when the difficult academic demands of college are considered, it's no wonder some student-athletes struggle to balance their studies with their sports.

NO BED OF ROSES

Student-athletes not only deal with confusing messages and hectic schedules, but they also must face the perceptions of other people. These perceptions can be positive toward the student-athlete or negative, but they are nearly always misguided.

Some student-athletes receive favored treatment and are given passing grades they don't deserve by teachers whose love of sports overshadows their integrity and honesty. In other cases, athletic department members or other teachers pressure a teacher to give an athlete a passing grade. Concern for the school's fortunes is greater than concern for the student-athlete's education.

Other high school and college student-athletes may be the victims of an anti-athletic backlash. Some teachers and professors don't expect much from student-athletes. A few have downright negative attitudes. Harry Edwards, a nationally known sports sociologist, maintains the American "dumb jock" picture is appealing to many people, including teachers. According to Edwards, this stereotype includes several common images:

• The dumb jock only attends school to play sports.
• The dumb jock can't do well in the classroom.
• The dumb jock cares only about victories and having fun.
• The dumb jock doesn't care about his or her grades.[8]

Harry Edwards, a sports sociology professor, urges student-athletes to stay focused on classwork.

Compounding the typical dumb jock image are racist attitudes deeply rooted in American culture. Edwards says that along with the dumb jock caricature, African-American student-athletes must endure the myth of "innate black athletic superiority" and the racial stereotype of the "dumb Negro."[9] In other words, some people believe blacks run faster, jump higher, but think slower. All of these stereotypes are unfounded.

Some professors and teachers

resent all of the attention given to athletics. They believe money is wasted on athletics. Although few teachers and professors go out of their way to make things difficult for student-athletes, some instructors don't respect the classroom efforts of student-athletes.

According to NCAA reports, more than half (55 percent) of college football and basketball players claim that teachers don't take them seriously as students. And 38 percent of student-athletes in other sports feel their studies are not taken seriously by professors. These two figures are much greater than the percentage (13 percent) of nonathletes who report their academic efforts not receiving the proper respect.[10]

One college football player put it this way: "I think there is a lot of discrimination toward student-athletes by faculty members of the campus. The other day I went to my teacher and he treated me like a BUM! He had a notion that I was there to beg for a better grade. I just went in for help and

to show I really took pride in my academics . . ." A female basketball player echoes those feelings: "People at this school generally look down on athletes. They consider us to be inferior on an intellectual level and many students feel that we are unworthy of attending this school. Personally, I am sick of this stereotypical view of 'jocks'."[11]

Why do some educators look down their noses at student-athletes? Certainly, the money and attention devoted to sports has much to do with it. But former University of Georgia faculty member Jan Kemp thinks there is more to it. Says Kemp, "There are so many professors in this nation—English professors are the world's worst—who say, 'We can't do anything with these [students] who are so deficient. We've got to accept only those who already have skill and talent.' Well, that's blatant bigotry."[12]

Jan Kemp, an assistant professor of developmental studies, was fired by the University of Georgia for protesting preferential treatment of athletes. She was reinstated in 1986.

A VICIOUS CYCLE

Considering the inconsistent messages sent by society, unrealistic expectations, time conflicts, and the negative feelings and stereotypes, no wonder some athletes begin to doubt themselves as students. Student-athletes may question their own role as a student. If teachers, relatives, and friends ask them only about their sports performances, not their studies, they might assume studying isn't that important. When deciding how to spend their time—whether studying, socializing, or practicing—student-athletes might be tempted by the short-term benefits of socializing or practicing over the long-term benefits of studying.[13]

The mixed bag of feelings and emotions about academics can cause stress for student-athletes.

Washington State University researchers conducted a study in 1987 of the self-perceptions of student-athletes and the stress they experienced. The study revealed many student-athletes weren't prepared for their studies.

For instance, college freshmen student-athletes assumed that college classes would require about as much studying as their high school classes had, and most had studied fewer than five hours a week in high school. Some stu-

dent-athletes decided schoolwork was less important than athletic performance. They became un-motivated and disinterested in classes. Finally, many athletes simply didn't realize the importance of their education.[14]

Student-athletes who go to college with realistic athletic and academic goals, and who have the support of their relatives and friends for achieving both goals, are often able to maintain a balance. But some student-athletes enter into a vicious cycle. Since their athletic achievements are noticed and rewarded more visibly than their academic achievements, these student-athletes make their sports efforts a higher priority than their studies. This sometimes results in lower grades and poor academic effort, thus reinforcing negative stereotypes.

CHAPTER THREE

STUDENT, ATHLETE, OR BOTH?

■

Students, parents, teachers, and fans sometimes seem to think of a student-athlete as an athlete first and a student second. What are the facts about the academic success of high school and college student-athletes? Graduation rates, grade point averages, and test scores of student-athletes are often reported in newspapers and magazines. But are these figures accurate measures of academic success?

For many years, people have questioned the academic performances of student-athletes. As early as 1929, the Carnegie Foundation for the Advancement of Teaching studied the effects of athletic participation on students' academic success. The Carnegie researchers concluded that the practice of recruiting high school athletes to attend college should stop. The report stated, "the devotion of an undue proportion of time to training, the devices for putting a desirable athlete, but a weak scholar, across the hurdles of examinations—these ought to stop." Other inquiries occurred during this era, and by 1934, 41

different studies showed "nonathletes performed slightly better in schoolwork than did athletes."[1]

Academic and recruiting scandals in the late 1970s renewed interest in examining high school and college athletics. Horror stories of college athletes, who could play very well but couldn't read, shocked the nation. The case of Kevin Ross, who attended Creighton University, was a dramatic ex-

Kevin Ross developed his basketball skills while attending Creighton University, but after college, he had to attend another school to learn how to read.

ample. Ross played intercollegiate basketball for Creighton for four years. After his college eligibility was used up, Ross went back to elementary school to learn to read. Ross had been given passing grades throughout his time at Creighton to keep him eligible to play basketball, but he had not been educated. His story was told in national newspapers, magazines, and on television shows. The televised image of an adult learning to read with a group of young children outraged many people. The Ross episode focused attention on the dilemma of athletics versus academics.

The number of students who graduate from a school and the grade point averages of those students are two ways to measure the academic success of high schools and colleges. But making these comparisons can be tricky. Getting accurate graduation figures and test scores is difficult because researchers often must rely on information from the schools themselves. Also, graduating from one school is not necessarily the same as graduating from another school. Making an A in one class is not necessarily the same as making an A in another. And schools' graduation rates may vary because of many factors, from different admissions standards to the resources available to students.

GETTING A DIPLOMA

On the high school level, athletes appear to graduate at a higher rate than nonathletes. In 1989 the Women's Sports Foundation studied the effects of high school varsity sports participation. The study concluded that sports keep many people in school. Among the findings were "white athletes (female and male) had lower dropout rates than nonathletes in suburban and rural schools." Black male athletes in rural schools were "over four and a half times less likely to drop out than their nonathletic counterparts. Hispanic female athletes were three times less likely to drop out than nonathletes."[2] But urban high school athletes didn't graduate at a higher rate than nonathletes.[3]

Unfortunately, it is in urban high schools where the greatest dropout problems exist. More than 700,000 students (approximately 15 percent) drop out of American high schools each year. Dropout rates—based on the number of students who start

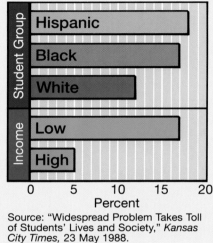

National Dropout Rates

These are the percentages of students, grouped by race and income level, who start school but don't graduate.

Source: "Widespread Problem Takes Toll of Students' Lives and Society," *Kansas City Times*, 23 May 1988.

school but do not graduate from high school—are particularly devastating in large cities. East Los Angeles has a dropout rate of nearly 60 percent. In Boston, a city known for its outstanding colleges and universities, nearly 50 percent of high school students drop out. Chicago has a high school dropout rate of more than 40 percent.[4]

Minority students make up a large number of those who leave high school early. Hispanic (18 percent) and black (17 percent) students have a higher national dropout rate than white students, who drop out at a 12 percent rate.

The gulf between nonpoor and poor is even wider. Poor students have a dropout rate of 17 percent nationally, compared to a 5 percent national rate for nonpoor students.[5] Many educators think that poverty is the number one reason for educational failure in the United States. Poor communities often cannot raise enough tax money to pay for good schools. Poor children often enter school at a disadvantage, and they often attend inferior schools.

EARNING A DEGREE

Most college student-athletes also do as well or better than students not playing sports. Fifty-five percent of all students entering NCAA Division I schools graduate within six years of enrollment. Student-athletes graduate at a higher rate than the overall student body—57 percent. In fact, women athletes do much better than their non-athletic peers. While 68 percent of female student-athletes earn a degree, just 57 percent of women who don't play organized sports graduate.[6]

Although the overall graduation rates for male student-athletes

Kim Gonzalez recorded more victories (33) than any other college softball pitcher in 1993 while she was a senior at Texas A&M University.

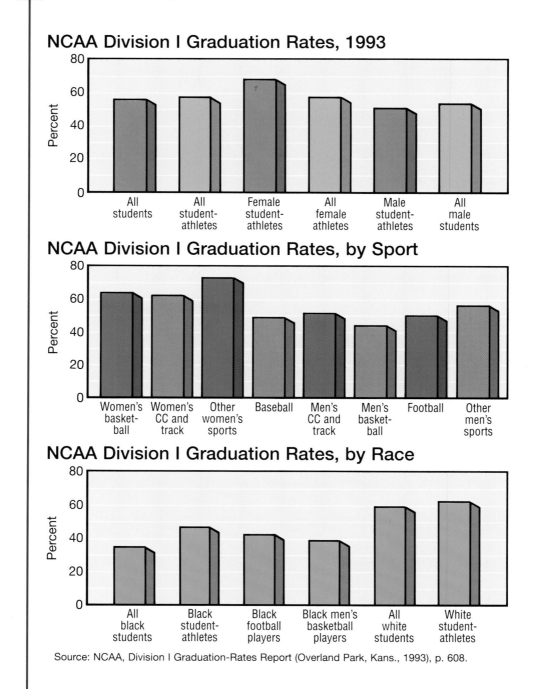

NCAA Division I Graduation Rates, 1993

NCAA Division I Graduation Rates, by Sport

NCAA Division I Graduation Rates, by Race

Source: NCAA, Division I Graduation-Rates Report (Overland Park, Kans., 1993), p. 608.

and male students in general are similar, the graduation rates for Division I men's basketball and football players are a different story. Male basketball players graduate at a rate of 44 percent, and football players graduate at a rate of 51 percent. Both of these graduation rates lag behind the 55-percent rate for all students.

Even more disturbing are the graduation rates for black male students. Black male basketball players graduate at a 38-percent rate, and black male football players graduate at a rate of 42 percent. Still, these rates are higher than the 30-percent graduation rate for all black male students at Division I institutions.[7]

MAKING THE GRADE

Grade point averages are another widely used measure of academic success. As with graduation rates, the overall grade point averages of student-athletes seem to dispel the dumb jock myth.

The Women's Sports Foundation report "found no evidence that sports participation was a detriment to getting good grades [in high school]. In fact, varsity athletes reported achieving higher averages than nonathletes." The

study found sports involvement was definitely linked to higher grades for rural Hispanic females, suburban black males, and rural white males.[8]

Achievement tests were another area where high school student-athletes did better than nonathletes. Minority student-athletes outperformed minority nonathletes in tests measuring mathematics, reading, and vocabulary. The Women's Sports Foundation report found more high test scores among athletes in all race and sex categories than nonathletes.[9] But the study noted that test score differences were due more to social and economic backgrounds than to sports participation itself.[10]

Although high school student-athletes seem to do as well or better than nonathletes with their grades, the grade point averages for college student-athletes do not compare so favorably. NCAA studies show "student-athletes in general have slightly lower cumulative GPAs in college than [nonathletes]."[11]

A 1986 study of a Division I school found that football and male basketball players had an average GPA of 2.25 on a 4.00 scale. This was lower than the 2.47

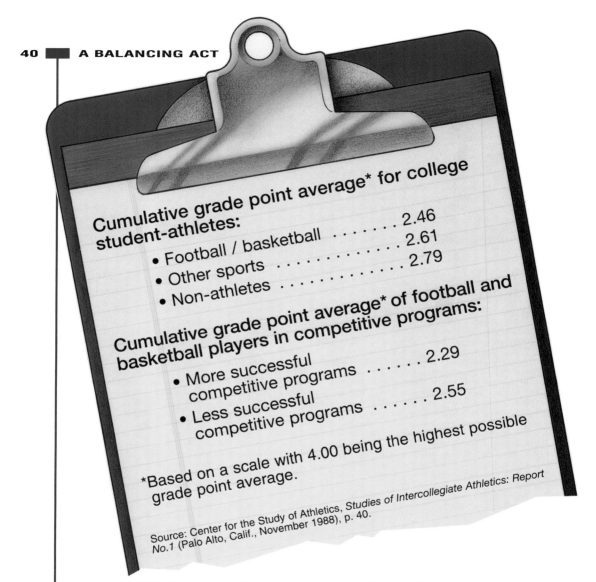

Cumulative grade point average* for college student-athletes:

- Football / basketball 2.46
- Other sports 2.61
- Non-athletes 2.79

Cumulative grade point average* of football and basketball players in competitive programs:

- More successful competitive programs 2.29
- Less successful competitive programs 2.55

*Based on a scale with 4.00 being the highest possible grade point average.

Source: Center for the Study of Athletics, Studies of Intercollegiate Athletics: Report No.1 (Palo Alto, Calif., November 1988), p. 40.

average GPA for males in other sports and the 2.57 average GPA for all university students. On the other hand, the report found that female student-athletes had a much higher grade point average (2.86) than the other reporting groups.[12] A 10-year (1970-1980) study of intercollegiate athletics in Colorado also found female student-athletes had a higher average GPA than other students.[13]

College football and male basketball players have the lowest grade point averages. And, players on winning football and men's basketball teams have average lower GPAs than players on less successful teams.[14]

Football and men's basketball have traditionally been termed *revenue sports,* that is sports from which colleges and universities make money. Perhaps the emphasis on winning and selling tickets in these sports encourages coaches and players to sacrifice studies for the benefit of sports success.

Also, the revenue sports have professional leagues. Athletes in these sports may be tempted to focus on their sports instead of their studies. These male basketball, football, and hockey players may see professional sports as a career choice. Athletes in nonrevenue sports, meanwhile, have fewer professional opportunities. They may think of their sports ability as a way of getting a college education to prepare them for other careers.

PROPOSITION 48

Efforts by the NCAA or state high school organizations to toughen academic requirements for student-athletes are controversial. If tougher grade-point average requirements are adopted, some

people argue, they will discriminate against poor and minority student-athletes. If higher college entrance exam scores are required for freshmen to play sports, critics claim, those standards would be unfair to students who traditionally score lower on these types of tests. Like dominoes falling one after another, each new rule may have an unsavory side effect.

A committee of 40 college presidents was formed in 1982 to solve the problems of "recruitment violation, illegal payments to student-athletes, tampering with academic records, and other irregularities."[15] Derek Bok, president of Harvard University, chaired the committee, which presented its proposals to the 1983 NCAA convention. Although the committee's proposals were softened somewhat, they eventually were accepted. The revised rules are known as Proposition 48 because that was the number by which they were introduced to NCAA delegates.

Of all the changes made in college athletics, Proposition 48 may be the NCAA's most controversial reform. Proposition 48 set standard entrance and eligibility requirements for all high school seniors planning to compete for

NCAA Division I schools. The rule said that all prospective student-athletes must have a minimum grade-point average of 2.0 in a set number of core classes, and a minimum score for the American College Testing Assessment (ACT) or Scholastic Assessment Test (SAT) college admissions tests. Student-athletes had to meet both requirements to play during their freshmen seasons. If an athlete didn't meet the standards, he or she could not receive a college scholarship without losing a year of eligibility or first graduating from a junior college.

A whole new set of labels was created by Proposition 48. Prospective student-athletes were either "qualifiers," "partial qualifiers" (they had made the GPA but not the test score), or they were "nonqualifiers" (they could not play for a Division I school).

Schools began to use Proposition 48 standards in 1986. The new rules got mixed reviews. Some educators said Proposition 48 helped to restore academic integrity to intercollegiate sports. J. W. Petalson, former president of the University of Illinois, said "We have a clear and inescapable responsibility to assert the supremacy of academic values."[16]

A QUESTION OF FAIRNESS

Critics of Proposition 48 agreed with the intent but questioned the method. Many educators and coaches believed basing eligibility on a single test score was unfair to many students, particularly minority students from poor backgrounds. These critics claim that the tests are written primarily by middle-class white people who have no knowledge of or experience with African-American or Hispanic cultures. The argument claims the language and references used by these tests favor the middle and upper classes, which are overwhelmingly white, and discriminate against blacks and other minorities.

Said John Chaney, Temple University basketball coach, in his critique of Proposition 48, "You're talking about predominantly blacks. You're not talking about anyone else."[17] Chaney's suspicions were well founded. Out of the first 400 student-athletes failing to meet the new standards, 85 percent were black.

Proposition 48 rules were revised to include a sliding scale rewarding high school athletes for high grade point averages. Still, a major change had been made. Prospective student-athletes would

Georgetown University men's basketball coach John Thompson has been a vocal critic of Proposition 48. He once boycotted a game to protest the rule, which he considers unfair to minority students.

have to meet uniform standards in grade point averages and standardized test scores. The rule had sent a wake-up call to high school coaches, counselors, and players.

NCAA PRESIDENTS' COMMISSION

Although Proposition 48 may be the most famous NCAA reform measure, several other pieces of legislation were enacted during the early 1990s. Many of these reforms were sponsored by the NCAA Presidents' Commission, formed in 1989. Composed of university presidents, the commission was created by NCAA members who were afraid the federal government would take over college sports. The purpose of the Presidents' Commission was to give university presidents

All student-athletes who want to play in NCAA Division I athletic programs must:

☑ Graduate from high school.

☑ Present a minimum combined **test score** on the **SAT** verbal and math sections or a minimum composite score on the **ACT** as indicated below:

Core GPA	SAT	ACT
2.500 and above	700	17
2.375	750	18
2.250	800	19
2.125	850	20
2.000	900 and above	21 and above

☑ Present a minimum **grade point average** in at least **13 core courses** in the following areas:

Course Title	No. of years
English	3
Mathematics	2
Natural or physical science	2
Additional courses in the above areas	2
Additional academic courses	2

Source: 1993-94 NCAA Guide for the College-Bound Student-Athlete

more ways to control college athletics programs.

The commission advocated a variety of changes, including:

• Mandatory in-season practice and competition time was limited to 20 hours per week and 4 hours a day. Athletes were guaranteed one day off per week.
• Athletic dormitories were to be eliminated and athlete-only training table meals were to be reduced to one per day by 1996 to keep from isolating the athletes.
• Coaching staffs were cut by at least one position in most sports.
• Athletic scholarships were reduced in all Division I sports.
• Division I athletes entering their fourth year of competition must have completed at least 50 percent of degree requirements to remain eligible.[18]

These rules seemed superficial to some, but they were intended to cut costs, make student-athletes more a part of the student body, and improve the image of college athletics. Hunter R. Rawlings III, the president of the University of Iowa, went as far as to state, "Now that the presidents have discovered how to reform intercollegiate athletics, we have no further excuses for scandal and failure."[19]

Although most of these changes were applauded, many critics claimed they did not go far enough. Many people called for more radical steps, including denying admission to athletes who are unqualified to do college-level work.

PASS TO PLAY

Many state high school associations have already adopted "Pass to Play" rules. This type of rule simply means high school student-athletes must pass their courses to play high school-sponsored sports. Many education groups, such as the National Association of Secondary School Principals, support these stricter rules.

Other educators, however, have criticized these regulations as being discriminatory against students from low-income families. These critics contend that poor students don't do as well in school because of limited resources. A "flunk and you're out" policy denies these students a chance to play sports, according to some. Athletics, claim these educators, may be the only reason some poor students stay in school.

IS REDSHIRTING FAIR?

Redshirting—legal and common on the college level—may give some high school student-athletes an unfair edge over their opponents. If an athlete is redshirted, that player repeats a grade and sits out a year to gain another season of eligibility. In other words, a student would actually attend high school five years and only play four of those years. The obvious advantage is players who redshirt have another year in which to become bigger, stronger, and faster. Some parents of junior high or high school athletes believe an extra year gives their sons or daughters an advantage in terms of age, strength, and speed. They hope this advantage will turn into a lucrative college scholarship.

Critics of the practice don't think 17-year-olds should have to compete against bigger and more physically mature 19-year-olds. Many state high school athletic organizations have made the practice of redshirting illegal. High school officials think redshirting is another example of de-emphasizing academics for athletics. Unfortunately, redshirt cases are not always so easily categorized. Many students have had to miss a year of sports for other, legitimate reasons.

Herman Jordan is one example.

Herman attended Chicago's Marshall High School. He was a good basketball player, but a poor student. More than half of his grades were Fs, and only one grade was better than a C. Herman dropped out of school during his junior year in 1990. He wasn't the only one to do that. By the time he dropped out, 437 of his 823 classmates had already dropped out.

Herman's mother was in poor health, and she was concerned about their neighborhood and its gangs, violence, and drug abuse. Because of her concerns, she sent Herman to live with an aunt in Fort Wayne, Indiana. Herman began his junior year again in 1991 at Fort Wayne's Snider High School. His attendance was excellent, and his grades began to improve.

According to the *Phi Delta Kappan* magazine, Herman's new principal described him as an "excellent example" for other students. Herman's basketball abilities also flourished. He started on his high school team, and he earned all-conference honors. Herman was looking forward to an outstanding senior season in the classroom and on the court.

Herman Jordan's dreams apparently ended, though, when the Indi-

Herman Jordan

eight semesters. Because Herman had dropped out of Marshall High in Chicago in mid-year, he had not received any academic credit for his junior year but he had used up two semesters of basketball eligibility. Therefore, with his senior season, Herman would be beginning his ninth semester. He was ineligible to play basketball.

Indiana's rule, like many similar rules in other states, was established to prevent high school students from redshirting. Herman Jordan's case was not so simple. Was Herman taking advantage of the system?

On December 10, 1992, Herman Jordan and his attorney filed suit against the Indiana High School Interscholastic Athletic Association for limiting his eligibility. After a two-month process—well into the basketball season—a federal court ruled in favor of Herman and his right to participate in the remainder of the Snider High School basketball season. Should the court have ruled in favor of Herman Jordan? Are rules on eligibility too rigid? If exceptions are made, are the rules weakened?

ana High School Interscholastic Athletic Association declared him ineligible to play basketball during his senior season. This ruling was based on the Indiana rule limiting high school athletic eligibility to

Source: Perry A. Zirkel, "Courts and Sports," *Phi Delta Kappan,* October 1993, pp. 188–189.

The San Francisco Giants agreed to pay outfielder Barry Bonds nearly $50 million dollars for playing baseball.

CHAPTER FOUR

HITTING PAY DIRT

■

Chris Webber, former star basketball player for the University of Michigan, signed a 15-year, $75 million dollar contract with the Golden State Warriors of the National Basketball Association in 1993. Barry Bonds, National League Most Valuable Player and outfielder for the San Francisco Giants, has a multiyear contract worth nearly $50 million dollars. Million-dollar contracts have become so common among pro athletes that only the most outrageous create a stir. No wonder so many high school and college athletes dream of playing professional sports. The rich contracts and constant television exposure are enough to lure almost anyone.

Unfortunately, the odds of playing professional athletics are slim. Only 8 percent of the student-athletes in college baseball, basketball, and football who are eligible for professional drafts each year are actually chosen by teams. Once players are drafted, very few actually play professionally. Even if they do get this rare opportunity, the average career lasts only three to four years.[1]

For example, there are 30 teams in the National Football League

Shaquille O'Neal left Louisiana State University before getting his degree to sign with the Orlando Magic of the National Basketball Association.

(NFL). Each team has a roster of 45 and a practice squad (a small group of alternate players) earning smaller paychecks. This means only 1,400 or so men are making a living playing NFL football during any given year. Combine this relatively small number with an average NFL career of only 3.2 years,[2] and the risk of relying on a professional football career is obvious. (A few other professional football leagues, such as the Canadian Football League and the Arena Football league exist, but their impact on these numbers is slight.) Despite this harsh reality, a 1988 NCAA study found that 23 percent of football and basketball players and 30 percent of student-athletes in other sports expected to become pro athletes.

This expectation may be particularly common among young black males. Those young blacks who live in poor, inner-city communities may view professional sports as the only way out of a dismal situation. Televised games and the constant barrage of advertisements only heighten this sense of escape. Images of Michael Jordan soaring through the galaxy to sell Nike shoes, Shaquille O'Neal knocking down gates to promote Pepsi, and Charles Barkley in animated battles with Godzilla bring the success and glory of successful black athletes into the homes of millions of African-American youngsters. Just watching the games

Many corporations pay former basketball star Michael Jordan millions of dollars to endorse their products.

National Basketball Association games, such as this one between the Minnesota Timberwolves and the Utah Jazz, showcase the athletic talents of black players.

themselves suggests pro sports are a haven for black athletes. Many National Basketball Association games will have 10 black players on the court at the same time. More than half of the football players in the NFL are black.

Sports sociologist Harry Edwards and other critics believe this expectation is nothing short of a hoax. They admit the percentage of black professional athletes is high (NBA, 74 percent; NFL, 55 percent; major league baseball, 19 percent), but they emphasize that only a tiny minority of blacks ever make it in pro sports. Even if coaching positions and trainers are included, according to Edwards, no more than 2,400 blacks make their living through professional sports. Edwards says many black athletes become "victims of a dream that has become a perpetual nightmare of futility and disappointment, holding to the hope of professional stardom until age and despair compel them to face the realities of life after sports."[3]

If young athletes ignore their studies in favor of pursuing a career as a pro athlete, chances are good that they will find themselves without the sports career and without the skills and education to pursue another career. But what about using those athletic skills to get a college degree? The opportunity to attend a college or university on a scholarship can be a benefit of high school athletic participation. The chances of a student getting a college scholarship are certainly better than his or her chances of becoming a pro athlete. Nearly 2,000 American universities and colleges have in-

tercollegiate athletics programs. Most of these schools give athletic scholarships in the many sports they sponsor.

THE LURE OF THE SCHOLARSHIP

Even for the talented athlete, the odds of receiving a full-ride scholarship aren't good. The full ride is a scholarship that pays for tuition, room, board, and books. (Athletic scholarships can't provide laundry money, weekend spending money, or car payments.) Full rides are only given to the most talented athletes. And then, with the exception of large Division I universities, full rides are often given only to football and basketball players.

For example, there are 294 Division I schools that compete in basketball. Each school is permitted 26 full scholarships—13 each for its men's and women's teams. This means about 7,600 student-athletes are receiving basketball scholarships to attend Division I institutions. Although 7,600 is a lot of people, it pales when compared to the 919,000 students who play high school basketball every year. Sometimes student-athletes are given partial scholarships.

ATHLETE, WITH A CAPITAL A

Frank Baker, University of Chicago economics major and football player, may be the perfect example of a scholar-athlete. In 1993, Baker set University of Chicago career records for rushing attempts (855), rushing yards (4,283), and total offense (4,350). Baker also served as one of the team captains.

But it was Baker's academic performance that made him truly special. Described by *Sports Illustrated* writer Rick Telander as a "bruising fullback with the brains of a college professor," Frank Baker was a Rhodes scholar candidate with a 3.7 grade point average at one of the toughest colleges in the country. He has already worked as an investment banker during his summer breaks, and he hopes to some day form a foundation to help hundreds of kids with their educations. As University of Chicago football coach Greg Quick said, "Frank is a great role model."

Source: Rick Telander, "Frank Baker," *Sports Illustrated,* 15 November 1993, p. 92.

This is particularly true for athletes in nonrevenue sports.

Some schools use partial scholarships to attract students. For example, a small private school may offer several thousand dollars of financial aid to a fairly good high school athlete. The student-athlete and his or her family must pay the rest of the tuition, which may be quite expensive.

Ivy League schools (Harvard University, Yale University, Princeton University, and others) do not give financial aid based on athletic ability. These are some of the best academic schools in the nation, and, as such, they are able to attract top-notch students because of their outstanding academic reputations.

Division III schools also don't give athletic scholarships. These schools don't emphasize competitive sports. While many Division III schools sponsor many teams and some have great athletic success, the Division III focus is not on drawing great crowds and making money.

An athletic scholarship is still a tremendous benefit to a student-athlete fortunate enough to receive it. The value of an athletic scholarship varies from college to college. The dollar amount changes with the annual tuition. Bucknell College, in Pennsylvania, for example, has an annual tuition of $14,800. This figure is almost 10 times as high as Montana State University's $1,526.[4]

PAYING FOR SCHOOL

For many years, sports enabled many students to attend college. Athletic scholarships provided the means for students who otherwise could not have paid the tuition. Two events made the sports-as-the-ticket-to-college practice obsolete. The GI Bill, along with Pell Grants, provided almost all eligible students with the means to attend college. *GI,* meaning government issue, became the generic term for military during World War II. At the end of World War II and during and after the Korean War, the GI Bill sent thousands of returning soldiers to colleges and universities on government money. In the 1960s, Pell Grants and student loan programs grew to the extent where millions of women and minority students were able to attend college. Pell Grants and similar programs were initiated by acts of the U.S. Congress.

Many supporters of college

WAYS TO PAY

Here are some sources of money for college:

Institutional funds: Most colleges offer grants, scholarships, loan programs, or student employment opportunities.

Pell Grants: Sponsored by the federal government, Pell Grants may be as much as $2,000 a year, based on families' financial needs.

College Work Study Programs: These programs provide campus-sponsored jobs for students who need financial aid.

National Direct Student Loan Program: This federal program provides loans to students. The loans must be repaid with 4 percent interest.

Guaranteed Student Loan Program: These loans come from many sources. The federal government pays full interest while the student is in college. After college, the student must repay the loan with interest.

Source: Richard Lapchick, *On the Mark* (Lexington, Mass.: Lexington Books, 1987), pp. 135–141.

athletics still claim sports scholarships are the only way for poor students to afford college. This view is an exaggeration. Financial aid packages and the vast number of low-cost community colleges mean any academically eligible student can continue his or her education after high school.

JUCO JUNGLE

NCAA academic rules have sent many student-athletes to junior, or two-year, colleges. Many junior colleges run outstanding programs. The men's basketball team from Labette Community College of Kansas had a team grade point average of 3.1 in 1994. In fact, a report in the *Chronicle of Higher Education* noted that many junior colleges take "academic rejects" and turn them into better "students and basketball players."[5]

But some junior colleges exploit student-athletes simply for their athletic skills. Harry Edwards believes the junior college system takes advantage of black student-athletes. Edwards estimates as many as 35 percent of black athletes talented enough for Division I athletic scholarships cannot receive them because of poor grades or test scores. Many of these athletes, according to Edwards, go to junior colleges to get the necessary grades to transfer to four-year schools. Edwards contends some junior college class work doesn't educate the student.

Some players are placed in junior colleges by brokers. Brokers are go-betweens who often receive money or other favors for bringing together students and junior colleges. The role of brokers has been criticized by many. Edwards refers to this system as nothing more than a "slave trade."[6] A former University of Houston assistant coach is also harsh in his criticism: "The brokers are like leeches. They're just high-class pimps."[7]

THROWING AWAY CAREERS

Whether in high school, junior college, or college, concentrating too much on sports can hurt a student's preparation for a non-athletic job. This issue is important in a world where the economy is changing. There are 35,000 job titles today in the United States, and futurists are predicting over half of the jobs in the next century do not yet exist![8]

The jobs of tomorrow are likely to require high levels of skills and abilities. Technology is becoming more sophisticated, and high-paying factory jobs are disappearing. There will be two kinds of jobs in the future: those requiring little or no skills, and those requiring strong qualifications. People with strong backgrounds in technology will have many job opportunities. Student-athletes who disregard their education in hopes of playing professionally may eventually have regrets.

PSYCHOLOGICAL PAYOFF, OR COST, OF SPORTS

But if a student-athlete decides to stay in school and learn, does his or her sports participation make the stay more enjoyable? More rewarding? More fun? Or more hassle?

Sports affects people's lives in different ways. Normally mild-mannered adults can turn into screaming fanatics when their children are involved in games of one kind or another. The effects of people's obsession with sports are obvious. The psychological impact of the same obsession upon student-athletes, however, is sometimes more difficult to gauge.

Many athletes compete in sports because they enjoy the experience. They like the physical activity and the opportunity to become better. Also, many athletes enjoy the camaraderie and companionship of being on a team. Lasting friendships can be formed by people who together endured the pain of practice, the joy of victory, and the disappointment of defeat.

Awards and occasionally seeing one's photograph in the newspaper are incentives. At some sports-oriented schools, athletes may become well known on campus and in the community. These honors may create a sense of greater popularity or power. The Women's Sports Foundation report found that high school athletes may work harder at school because they feel they fit in there.

A 1988 Studies of Intercollegiate Athletics study compared the opportunities for personal growth between college student-athletes and nonathletes. Personal growth was divided into four categories: leadership and personal development, sociability, assertiveness, and rewards and recognition from others.

The study found that student-athletes have more difficulty assuming leadership roles and accepting responsibility for others than do nonathletes. The study also found that student-athletes gained fewer benefits from "social interactions" than nonathletes. Only 35 percent of football and basketball players believe "it is 'easier' or 'much easier' for them to be liked for just being themselves." This figure compares to 61 percent for other students.

Only 40 percent of football and basketball players and 29 percent of other student-athletes were comfortable when speaking their minds, compared to 66 percent of students not participating in athletics. Football and basketball players reported it was easier for them to get special treatment from local people and merchants than it was for other students. There was no significant difference, however, between student-athletes and nonathletes in the area of earning praise or recognition for abilities.

The Studies of Intercollegiate Athletics also explored the subject of physical and mental abuse. Most students and student-athletes reported never experiencing any physical or mental abuse. Nearly 20 percent of Division I basketball and football players claim to have been physically abused compared to 10 percent for other student-athletes and 8 percent for nonathletes. Nearly half of the college football and basketball players interviewed reported mental abuse (yelling, putdowns, degradation), compared to 39 percent for other student-athletes and 38 percent for nonathletes.[9]

Consider the comments of a female student-athlete interviewed for this study: "I would like to describe my personal experiences with a threatening, terrible coach. The coach I had my freshman year shook my confidence and self-esteem so much that I feel it has taken me three years to regain most of it. She continually threatened me with my scholarship, told me my friends and family disliked me, and generally made me miserable."[10]

Interestingly, the rates for physical and mental abuse were higher for athletes in successful football and basketball programs than for those in less successful programs. Football and basketball players "in more successfully competitive programs also are more likely to report feelings of isolation from other students than are participants in less successfully competitive programs."[11]

STANDING OUT

Feelings of isolation have been felt by thousands of college students. And racial discrimination adds to the burden of black athletes. Although 12 percent of the U.S. population is black, blacks comprise only 4 percent of American college enrollment. The NCAA says more than half of black Division I football and basketball players report feeling racially isolated. One-third of these athletes reported racial discrimination.[12]

As one black college football player said, "It's hard to adjust to the environment I'm in because I'm black. It's a big difference from home. People look and stare at me sometimes as though I'm an animal. Sometimes I can't stand it. If someone black gets in trouble, people around here say it was an athlete. This is something I can't stand."[13]

CHAPTER FIVE

THE PAYOFF FOR SCHOOLS

■

Supporters of athletic programs often say that sports teams are good for schools. Some college presidents have claimed private donations begin on the 50-yard line. Public school superintendents have gone on record as saying voters will agree to raise taxes to pay for school improvements if the school athletic teams are winning. The general public believes schools, colleges in particular, make a lot of money from ticket sales and television contracts.

Another often-cited benefit of athletic programs is the positive publicity sports teams give high schools or colleges. Winning teams grab newspaper headlines, local and national television coverage, and praise from politicians and community leaders. Again, many school leaders believe this type of attention is excellent for the school's reputation and attracts donations and more students.

The involvement of support groups is seen as another positive aspect of athletic programs. Athletics aren't just for the players and coaches. Cheerleaders, band members, student managers, and spectators are all part of athletic events. Football on Friday nights

and Saturday afternoons provide exciting entertainment for millions of fans every fall.

Sports have their critics, though. Many people believe sports teams are a waste of time and money. These people claim that many university athletic programs lose millions of dollars each year. Others not in favor of sports believe all the attention given to athletics emphasizes the wrong values. They don't think successful teams help the academic programs of high schools and colleges, and they challenge those who do think so to prove it. Finally, some people think athletics' contribution to school spirit and general student involvement is overrated. Clearly, deciding whether high schools and colleges actually benefit from sponsoring athletic programs demands a close and careful look at the money, at schools' reputations, and at the actual level of student and community involvement in sports programs.

BIG BUCKS OR BIG BUST?

The finances of high school and college athletics are quite different. Few high schools actually make money by sponsoring sports events, and high school athletic

High school athletic contests often draw smaller crowds than college events.

WHAT'S THE DIFFERENCE?

Basic differences between high school and college sports programs:

HIGH SCHOOLS	COLLEGES AND UNIVERSITIES
• No athletic scholarships.	• Each school, except in Division III, may give athletic scholarships.
• Coaches usually teach classes and receive relatively little pay for coaching.	• Coaches often do not teach classes. Many successful coaches in basketball and football receive huge salaries and bonuses.
• Coaches rarely receive cars.	• Coaches in revenue sports almost always receive cars
• There are a few low-paid assistant coaches.	• There are often several well-paid assistant coaches.
• Recruiting players to public schools is not allowed.	• Coaches spend vast sums of money recruiting talented players to come to their colleges.
• Travel is usually local and done on a bus.	• Travel is often far-flung and is sometimes done on airplanes.
• Coaches often handle such things as scheduling, media, and laundry.	• Specialists are hired by college athletic departments to promote games, raise funds, and do other administrative duties.

programs are relatively cheap. In contrast, hundreds of colleges and universities make huge sums of money from sports, and the costs of running their athletic programs are tremendous.

Most high school athletic departments spend from $20,000 to $100,000, depending on the size of the school. University athletic departments, on the other hand, may spend as little as $400,000 or

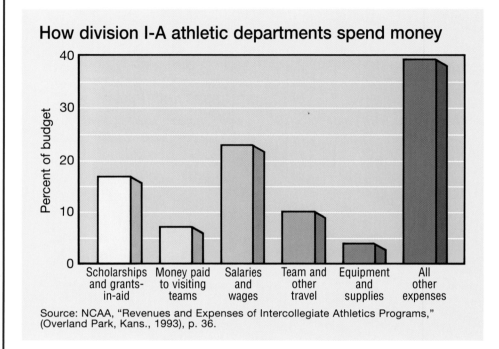

How division I-A athletic departments spend money

Source: NCAA, "Revenues and Expenses of Intercollegiate Athletics Programs," (Overland Park, Kans., 1993), p. 36.

as much as $22,000,000! University athletic departments spend these huge sums of dollars in various ways. The chart, above, shows where the money goes.

The highest category is, curiously, "All Other Expenses." According to the NCAA, this category includes "insurance, certain facility maintenance costs and general overhead expenses of the athletics department."[1] These "overhead expenses," which can include almost anything, are often targets for critics of college sports.

But looking only at the costs of athletics proves little. The amount of revenue compared to those costs is what determines whether an athletic program makes money. If the revenue is more than the expenses, the program is making money. If not, the program is losing money.

BALANCING THE BOOKS

High school sports programs don't make profits. There may be a rare exception in the football-crazy states of Texas, Florida, and Ohio where a high school football program sells enough tickets to support the rest of the athletic program. But in most cases, high school sports departments don't make more money than they spend.

Do colleges make money on sports? With all of the ticket sales, television revenues, concession stand proceeds, donations from alumni, and parking lot fees, it seems they should. The answer? It depends on which college you examine.

The common perception is that ticket sales and television monies are what pay the bills. But ticket sales account for only 35 percent of Division I-A revenues and even less at the smaller schools (as little as 2 percent at Division III schools not playing football). Television revenues make up only 14 percent of incoming athletic dollars at Division I-A schools and are virtually nonexistent at Division II and III institutions.[2]

The rest of the athletic department money comes from many

NCAA DIVISIONS

Division I: This division includes both Division I-A and Division I-AA. Division I-A schools play major college football and offer more football scholarships than Division I-AA schools, which compete in a separate football division. All other men's and women's sports are conducted together.

Division II: These colleges and universities are often smaller than Division I-A schools. These schools spend less on their athletic programs and are allowed fewer scholarships per sport than the larger Division I programs. NCAA Division II conducts national championships in all men's and women's sports.

Division III: These schools are often referred to as small colleges. Although Division III holds national tournaments in all men's and women's sports, no athletic scholarships are permitted.

sources—student activity fees, contributions from alumni, state support, and a category the NCAA calls "All Other Revenues".[3] The "All Other Revenues" category may include everything from bookstore profits to money collected from soda machines on campus. In fact, a university president may decide to use student tuition monies to fund sports teams. Whether student tuition should be considered athletic revenue is a matter for debate.

Most colleges don't make money from their sports departments. Even big-time Division I schools, such as the University of Michigan, the University of California at Los Angeles, the University of North Carolina, and other schools often featured on television, on the average only break even. In other words, their revenues barely cover their expenses.

Just looking at the average may be misleading, however. Although the NCAA reports the average Division I-A school has overall revenues of $9,685,000 and expenses of $9,646,000—which shows a very small profit—only the most successful programs actually make any money.[4]

While the University of Notre Dame, with its network football

Revenue Sources of the Various Athletic Divisions

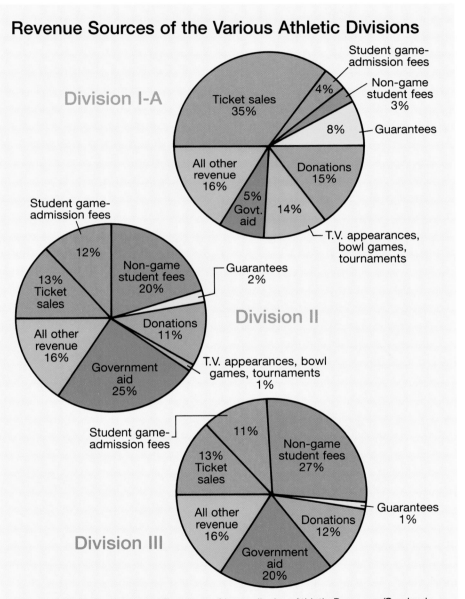

Source: NCAA, *Revenues and Expenses of Intercollegiate Athletic Programs* (Overland Park, Kans., October 1990), p. 17.

contract (with NBC), and other megaprograms like the University of Nebraska earn enormous profits, the majority of Division I-A schools struggle just to break even or they lose money each year. Even the highly successful University of Michigan has reported losses during past years.[5]

For smaller universities, athletics is simply a money-losing proposition. Division I-AA schools like Western Carolina, Harvard University, and North Texas State lose on average $782,000 a year. Division II schools (such as University of North Dakota, University of North Alabama, and California State University, Bakersfield) lose an average of $897,000, and Division III colleges (smaller schools like Coe College, Williams College, and Centre College) lose on average $400,000 each year.[6]

Individual Division I football and men's basketball teams can be lucrative, though. Because of ticket sales and television contracts, successful teams can bring in large sums of money. Successful is the key word, however, because in the NCAA, to the victors go the spoils.

It works like this. All college teams bring in varying amounts of revenues from ticket sales and donations. These earnings don't cover the overall costs of a university's expensive athletic program. The best way for an athletic program to increase its earnings is to go to a football bowl game or to advance in the NCAA National Championship men's basketball tournament. Bowl game teams receive huge sums of money for participating, and the amount of money an NCAA tourney team earns depends on how far it advances in the field of 64.

Critics of college sports believe this pressure to earn money by winning causes coaches to break the rules and downplay academics. The critics suggest revenue from bowl games, television contracts, and national tournaments should be shared equally by all NCAA members. Revenue sharing, according to some, would reduce the motivation to cheat or exploit student-athletes.

Revenue sharing occurs to some extent already, as many conferences such as the Big Ten, the Big Eight, and the Atlantic Coast Conference have revenue-sharing plans in place. Winning teams still get the most money in these conferences, though, and every year, the same teams dominate NCAA football and basketball competition.

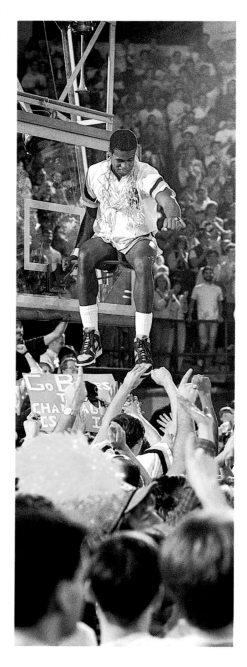

Many successful schools are opposed to equal revenue sharing for obvious reasons. It would reduce the amount of money they get. Smaller and less successful schools, on the other hand, bring up the revenue-sharing issue every year. They claim the NCAA system is simply a matter of the rich getting richer.

Many college presidents believe strong athletic programs encourage alumni and friends to give more money to various university programs. This belief seems sensible. Donations to athletic programs definitely increase when a university's teams win.

But do more donations for athletics carry over to academics? Murray Sperber, author of *College Sports, Inc.*, believes money raised because of athletic success is used for sports and rarely reaches classrooms. Although winning football teams sometimes are responsible for new stadiums, rarely are new biology labs built because a high school football team won a state championship. The NCAA report showing only 15 percent of NCAA Division I revenues coming from private donations seems to support this argument. There doesn't seem to be much money left over to share with academic programs.

Another study, published in 1994, however, found there was spillover. These researchers tracked the effect of athletic performance on alumni donations at a typical NCAA Division I school over a 30-year period. Their research showed that winning teams did seem to generate more gifts to the school and its academic programs. The study also found that greater television exposure increased giving.[7]

On the other hand, when Wichita State University dropped football, annual donations to that university nearly doubled in the years that followed. Even the University of Notre Dame saw an increase in academic donations during the early 1980s when its football teams were losing. Obviously, there isn't a firm correlation between how much money alumni give to a college and the school's athletic success.

ENHANCED REPUTATION

If high school and college athletic programs don't make money, does the positive publicity still make athletic programs worthwhile? Some sports advocates claim winning teams help a school's overall academic programs.

Schools certainly become more familiar to people through their sports teams. But do students base their choice of school on the success of high school or college athletic programs? Certainly, prospective student-athletes are interested in the quality of a school's teams. But what about the student who doesn't play a varsity sport and rarely, if ever, attends a sporting event? Undoubtedly, some private high schools have made a name for themselves by their success in a sport. Baltimore's DeMatha High, New York's Christ the King High School, and Virginia's Oak Hill Academy are known nationally because of their success in basketball. Millions of people were introduced to the University of Nevada, Las Vegas, and DePaul

University because of their success in college basketball. But proving without doubt students go to these schools because of athletic success is impossible.

Colleges such as Harvard, Yale, Princeton, Williams College, Rice, Northwestern, and University of Chicago are recognized as among the best in the nation. These schools haven't been to the Final Four or won a big-time bowl game in decades. Colleges and universities of this caliber, and the top academic high schools as well, don't rely on athletic championships to build their reputations. Their academic achievements stand by themselves.

FANS IN THE STANDS

The social lives of students in American high schools often center around the school's sports events. Often, many of a high school's students will be involved in the band, at the concession stands, in the cheering section, and as team managers. The big game on Friday is the reason for many dances, picnics, dates, and parties. Of course, the bigger the school and the greater the extracurricular options, the less the overall involvement of students in each activity will be. A high school with 400 students will have a greater sense of team spirit than a high school of 3,000 students.

The sense of participation is even less on the college level. At a university with 20,000 students, only a small fraction of students actually will be involved in the sports events themselves even though other students can buy tickets to the games. This is one

reason why huge athletic budgets have come under such scrutiny. Many people don't believe colleges should spend $15,000,000 on athletic programs involving several hundred students, and spend only $50,000 on the intramural programs for the thousands of students making up the rest of the student body.

Some people wonder if the benefits of sports participation could be extended to more students—particularly those in high schools—if some sports teams were made up of boys and girls. Perhaps schools could sponsor teams of boys and girls in such sports as racquetball, weightlifting, cycling, skiing, and rowing. Or perhaps student-athletes could be responsible for organizing and running their own sports activities with some guidance from a teacher or coach. Would this type of program encourage more students to participate, or would the elite athletes who compete in the current programs also dominate a student-run program?

CHAPTER SIX

THE NEXT MOVE?

■

Despite the many attempts to make school sports fairer and more honest, some people believe the rules do not go far enough. These people think the actual structure of school-sponsored team sports should be changed. Some of the suggestions include the creation of minor leagues in basketball and football, doing away with athletic scholarships, and restructuring the way college teams earn revenue.

CREATING MINOR LEAGUES

Professional football and basketball are blamed for many of the existing abuses in college sports. Critics say that pro sports have used colleges and universities as minor leagues without paying the expenses or accepting the responsibilities. The current situation results in many players going to college with no intention of studying. They go to college to play their sport. While on campus they become pseudo-students, playing the academic game to stay eligible—their only chance at making the NBA or NFL. This fraud makes a mockery of many universities' claims about athletes being students first.

Few players make NFL or NBA

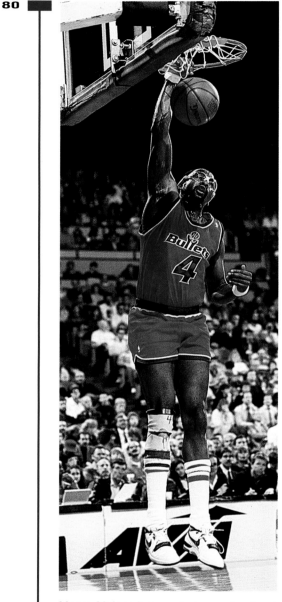

Moses Malone began playing professional basketball in 1974, right after completing high school in Virginia. His 20-year career includes a championship season with Philadelphia in 1983.

teams without playing in college. Two notable exceptions were Moses Malone, a former NBA Most Valuable Player with the Philadelphia 76ers, and Darryl Dawkins, a former New Jersey Net, who invented the technique of shattering backboards long before Orlando Magic superstar Shaquille O'Neal.

Professional baseball has always supported a minor league system, and college baseball, at least to this point, has avoided the academic and recruiting troubles found in men's basketball and football. Baseball players have the option of signing a professional contract and performing in the major league-sponsored minor league system. More and more professional baseball players are emerging from the college ranks, but an athlete who isn't interested in college can avoid the academic sham acted out by many college football and basketball players.

Several ways to implement the minor league system have been proposed. They range from basketball and football minor league systems apart from colleges, to placing professional farm teams on campuses where they would represent schools and states much as college teams do now.

Other critics think colleges should forget about amateurism and pay athletes for their labor. Rick Telander, author of *The Hundred Yard Lie,* has proposed an interesting solution. Telander supports an Age Group Professional Football League (AGPFL). The AGPFL would be similar to Canada's junior hockey system, and the league would have elements of baseball's minor league system. Major NCAA Division I universities wanting to retain big-time football would form the nucleus of the league. Telander estimates this would include 50 to 80 schools from the current major conferences. Teams

would keep team names and school mascots; existing university facilities would be used. The National Football League would fund the league by giving money to an AGPFL pool.

AGPFL players would not have to be students, even though they would "work" on college campuses. Players would have to be 18 to 22 years old and have a high school diploma. They would receive a reasonable salary, and they could earn incentives and bonuses. The players could attend university classes, but there would be no academic requirements.

Under Telander's plan, colleges and universities playing football but not participating in the AGPFL would be forced to limit the number of coaches, strengthen academic guidelines, and shorten seasons. In other words, traditional college football would be de-emphasized.[1]

DIVISION III MODEL

The Division III model is another approach to reforming intercollegiate athletics. Division III schools don't give athletic scholarships. Many Division III athletes receive financial aid, but it is based on need or academic performance.

Division III schools don't see intercollegiate sports as a way to make money. Division III schools view sports as an extracurricular activity for students. In fact, because of the low cost, many schools in NCAA Division III offer more sports than many Division I schools, thus providing more opportunities for students to participate. Swarthmore College, a Division III school in Pennsylvania, is an example. Swarthmore sponsors 24 sports. The University of Tulsa, a bigger "sports school," sponsors 13.[2] Division III sports are also competitive. National championships are held in all sports, and occasionally a former Division III student-athlete will succeed as a pro athlete.

STUDENTS FIRST

High school athletics and intercollegiate athletics have as many differences as similarities. Still, there are significant connections between the two. The national publicity heaped on college football and basketball makes high school events all the more important. The lure of getting a college athletic scholarship is the driving force behind the efforts of many high school athletes and their

Swarthmore College, a Division III school, offers its students a variety of sports, including lacrosse, in which to participate.

parents. The widespread calls for reforms in college sports infiltrated high school athletics in the form of "Pass to Play" and redshirting rules.

Understanding this relationship between high schools and colleges is important, but it solves no problems. Balancing athletics and academics remains difficult, and in America's sports-crazed society this will be true for years to come.

Richard E. Lapchick and his Northeastern University Center for the Study of Sport in Society have made a crusade of "putting the student back in the student-athlete." Lapchick believes high school athletes must know more

GRADING A COLLEGE

Richard E. Lapchick and the Northeastern University Center for the Study of Sport in Society advise student-athletes to consider the following factors when selecting a college:

- the climate

- the location and distance from home

- the size of school

- the housing and dining facilities

- academic support systems for student-athletes

- the social life on campus

- Does the school have the exact academic program a student is looking for?

Richard E. Lapchick

about the sometimes harsh realities of sports and academics. "Pro contracts are unrealistic for all but a few," says Lapchick, and high school student-athletes must learn how to prepare for college and select the right school."[3]

High school and college sports provide students with wonderful opportunities. Athletic events should provide healthy, vigorous, and exciting activities. The key is for student-athletes to keep academic priorities in perspective.

Solutions may never come from more rules, stronger organizations, or radical changes. Maybe only the efforts of individuals— athletes and their families—will bring about meaningful change. Perhaps it is student-athletes themselves who must accept the responsibility for finding and maintaining the proper balance.

NOTES

CHAPTER 1: BALANCING THE BALL: ATHLETICS AND ACADEMICS

1. "Division I-A Graduation Rates," *USA Today,* 3 June 1993, Sports section.

2. Phil Taylor, "Courted and Convicted," *Sports Illustrated,* 26 July 1993, pp. 26–27.

3. Shirley and Alfred Tamarin, *Olympic Games in Ancient Greece* (New York: Harper & Row, 1976), p. 26.

4. Richard M. Restak, *The Brain: The Last Frontier* (New York: Warner Books, 1979), p. 122.

5. Rick Telander, *The Hundred Yard Lie* (New York: Simon and Schuster, 1989), p. 32.

6. Richard O'Brien, "Scorecard," *Sports Illustrated,* 22 November 1993, p. 10.

7. Donald Chu, *The Character of American Higher Education and Intercollegiate Sport* (Albany, N.Y.: State University of New York Press, 1989), p. 53.

8. John Durant, *Yesterday in Sports* (New York: A. S. Barnes and Company, 1956), pp. 130–131.

9. Gary Funk, *Major Violation: The Unbalanced Priorities in Athletics and Academics* (Champaign, Ill.: Leisure Press, 1991), pp. 12–13.

10. Michael R. Steele, *Knute Rockne, A Bio-Bibliography* (Westport, Conn.: Greenwood Press, 1983), p. 34.

11. Steele, *Knute Rockne,* p. 20.

12. Steele, *Knute Rockne,* p. 36.

13. National Collegiate Athletic Association, *1993–94 NCAA Guide for the College-Bound Student-Athlete* (Overland Park, Kans., 1993).

14. G.H. Sage, *Power and Ideology in American Sport: A Critical Perspective* (Champaign, Ill.: Human Kinetics, 1990), p. 171.

15. Missouri State High School Activities Association, *1993–94 Official Handbook,* p. 7.

CHAPTER 2: ALL THINGS TO ALL PEOPLE

1. Joe Nathan, "TV School Coverage Sends Wrong Message," *St. Paul (Minnesota) Pioneer Press,* 6 September 1993, C section.

2. "Serious Sports," *School Administrator,* August 1993, p. 5.

3. Southwest Missouri State University Study Skills Report, 1989.

4. Center for the Study of Athletics, *Studies of Intercollegiate Athletics, Report No. 6* (Palo Alto, Calif., August 1989), p. 23. This study examined more than 4,000 students at 42 NCAA institutions.

5. Gib Twyman, "Geography Class Studies Team Travel," *Kansas City Star,* 24 September 1990.

6. Center for the Study of Athletics, *Studies of Intercollegiate Athletics, Report No. 6* (Palo Alto, Calif., August 1989), p. 23.

7. Ladell Anderson, "Starting Basketball After Christmas Makes Sense," *NCAA News,* 28 December 1988, p. 4.

8. Harry Edwards, "The Black Dumb Jock," *The College Board Review 131,* Spring 1984, p. 8.

9. Edwards, "The Black Dumb Jock," p. 8.

10. Center for the Study of Athletics, *Studies of Intercollegiate Athletics: Report No. 1,* p. 46.

11. Center for the Study of Athletics, *Studies of Intercollegiate Athletics, Report No. 6,* p. 45.

12. Chuck Reece, "Jan Kemp," *Ms.,* January 1987, p. 89.

13. Jay Coakley, *Sport In Society* (St. Louis, Mo.: Times Mirror/Mosby College Pub., 1994), pp. 398–400.

14. Janice Roberts-Wilbur, Michael Wilbur, and Joseph R. Morris, "The Freshman Athlete's Transition: Athletic and Academic Stressors," *Academic Athletic Journal,* Spring 1987, pp. 23–34.

CHAPTER 3: STUDENT, ATHLETE, OR BOTH?

1. Robert J. Ballantine, "What Research Says about the Correlation between Athletic Participation and Academic Achievement," U.S. Department of Education, Washington, D.C. ED233994, 1981, p. 2.

2. Women's Sports Foundation, *Minorities in Sports* (Northeastern University, August 1989), p. 4.

3. WSF, *Minorities in Sports,* p. 9.

4. Gary Funk, *Major Violation* (Champaign, Ill.: Human Kinetics, 1991), p. 58.

5. Tim O'Connor, "Widespread Problem Takes Toll on Students' Lives and Society," *Kansas City Times,* 23 May 1988.

6. National Collegiate Athletic Association, *Division I Graduation-Rates Report* (Overland Park, Kans., 1993), p. 608.

7. NCAA, *Division I Graduation-Rates Report,* p. 608.

8. WSF, *Minorities in Sports,* p. 8.

9. WSF, *Minorities in Sports,* p. 25.

10. WSF, *Minorities in Sports,* p. 8.

11. Center for the Study of Athletics, *Studies of Intercollegiate Athletics: Report No. 1* (Palo Alto, Calif., November 1988), p. 39.

12. Ann Mayo, "Athletes and Academic Performance: A Study of Athletes at an NCAA Division I Institution," *Academic Athletic Journal,* Spring 1986, pp. 27–30.

13. Timothy L. Walter, "Predicting the Academic Success of College Athletes," *Research Quarterly for Exercise and Sport 58,* 1987, p. 275.

14. Center for the Study of Athletics, *Studies of Intercollegiate Athletics: Report No. 1* (Palo Alto, Calif., November 1988), p. 40.

15. Funk, *Major Violation,* p. 108.

16. Linda Greene, "The New NCAA Rules of the Game: Academic Integrity or Racism," *St. Louis Law Journal* 28, 1984, p. 103.

17. Associated Press, "Prop 48 Claims Heavy Toll Among Black Athletes," *Kansas City Star,* 31 March 1989.

18. Steve Wulf, "Scorecard," *Sports Illustrated,* 21 January 1991, p. 9.

19. Hunter R. Rawlings III, "Why Did It Take So Long?" *Sports Illustrated,* 21 January 1991, p. 72.

CHAPTER 4: HITTING PAY DIRT

1. Harry Edwards, "The Black Dumb Jock," *The College Board Review 131,* Spring 1984, p. 9.

2. Edwards, "The Black Dumb Jock," p. 10.

3. Edwards, "The Black Dumb Jock," p. 9.

4. James Cass and Max Birnbaum, *Comparative Guide to American Colleges* (New York: Harper Perennial, 1991).

5. Charles S. Farrell, "Turning Academic Rejects into Students Who Also Play Top Basketball," *The Chronicle of Higher Education,* 25 March 1987, pp. 36–38.

6. Edwards, "The Black Dumb Jock," p. 9.

7. Alexander Wolf and Armen Keteyian, *Raw Recruits* (New York: Pocket Books, 1990), p. 45.

8. Jan Bradley, Gary Funk, JoBelle Hopper, and Myrna Walker Hyte, *Thrills, Spills, and Study Skills* (Dubuque, Iowa: Kendall-Hunt Publishers, 1992), p. 215.

9. Center for the Study of Athletics, *Studies of Intercollegiate Athletics: Report No. 1* (Palo Alto, Calif., November 1988), p. 55.

10. Center for the Study of Athletics, *Studies of Intercollegiate Athletics, Report No. 6* (Palo Alto, Calif., August 1989), p. 41.

11. Center for the Study of Athletics, *Studies of Intercollegiate Athletics: Report No. 1,* p. 55.

12. Center for the Study of Athletics, *Studies of Intercollegiate Athletics: Report No. 3,* (March 1989), p. 3.

13. Center for the Study of Athletics, *Studies of Intercollegiate Athletics, Report No. 6,* p. 58.

CHAPTER 5: THE PAYOFF FOR SCHOOLS

1. National Collegiate Athletic Association, *Revenues and Expenses of Intercollegiate Athletics Programs* (Overland Park, Kans., October 1990), p. 36.

2. NCAA, *Revenues and Expenses,* p. 17.

3. NCAA, *Revenues and Expenses,* p. 17.

4. NCAA, *Revenues and Expenses,* pp. 10, 30.

5. Gary Funk, *Major Violation* (Champaign, Ill.: Human Kinetics, 1991), p. 66.

6. NCAA, *Revenues and Expenses,* pp. 10, 30.

7. Paul W. Grimes and George A. Chressanthis, "Alumni Contributions to Academics: The Role of Intercollegiate Sports and NCAA Sanctions," *American Journal of Economics and Sociology, Vol. 53, No. 1* (January 1994), pp. 27–38.

CHAPTER 6: THE NEXT MOVE?

1. Rick Telander, *The Hundred Yard Lie* (New York: Simon & Schuster, 1989), pp. 213–215.

2. James Cass and Max Birnbaum, *Comparative Guide to American Colleges* (New York: Harper Perennial, 1991), pp. 585, 613.

3. Richard E. Lapchick, *On The Mark* (Lexington, Mass.: Lexington Books, 1987), p. 29.

BIBLIOGRAPHY

Anderson, Ladell. "Starting Basketball After Christmas Makes Sense." *NCAA News,* 28 December 1988.

Associated Press. "Prop 48 Claims Heavy Toll Among Black Athletes." *Kansas City Star,* 31 March 1989.

Ballantine, Robert J. "What Research Says about the Correlation between Athletic Participation and Academic Achievement." U.S. Department of Education, Washington, D.C., ED233994, 1981.

Bradley, Jan, and Gary Funk, JoBelle Hopper, and Myrna Walker Hyte. *Thrills, Spills, and Study Skills.* Dubuque, Iowa: Kendall-Hunt Publishers, 1992.

Cass, James, and Max Birnbaum. *Comparative Guide to American Colleges.* New York: Harper Perennial, 1991.

Center for the Study of Athletics. *Studies of Intercollegiate Athletics: Report No. 1.* Palo Alto, Calif., November 1988.

Center for the Study of Athletics. *Studies of Intercollegiate Athletics: Report No. 3.* Palo Alto, Calif., March 1989.

Center for the Study of Athletics. *Studies of Intercollegiate Athletics, Report No. 6.* Palo Alto, Calif., August 1989.

Chu, Donald. *The Character of American Higher Education and Intercollegiate Sport.* Albany, N.Y.: State University of New York Press, 1989.

Coakley, Jay. *Sport In Society.* St. Louis, Mo.: Times Mirror/Mosby College, 1994.

"Division I-A Graduation Rates." *USA Today,* 3 June 1993.

Durant, John. *Yesterday in Sports.* New York: A. S. Barnes and Company, 1956.

Edwards, Harry. "The Black Dumb Jock." *The College Board Review* 131, Spring 1984.

Farrell, Charles S. "Turning Academic Rejects into Students Who Also Play Top Basketball." *The Chronicle of Higher Education,* 25 March 1987.

Funk, Gary. *Major Violation: The Unbalanced Priorities in Athletics and Academics.* Champaign, Ill.: Leisure Press, 1991.

Greene, Linda. "The New NCAA Rules of the Game: Academic Integrity or Racism." *St. Louis Law Journal 28,* 1984.

Grimes, Paul W. and George A. Chressanthis. "Alumni Contributions to Academics: The Role of Intercollegiate Sports and NCAA Sanctions." *American Journal of Economics and Sociology,* Vol. 53, No. 1, January 1994.

Lapchick, Richard E. *On The Mark.* Lexington, Mass.: Lexington Books, 1987.

Masin, Herman L. "A Knight in Gettysburg." *Scholastic Coach,* August 1991.

Mayo, Ann. "Athletes and Academic Performance: A Study of Athletes at an NCAA Division I Institution." *Academic Athletic Journal,* Spring 1986.

Missouri State High School Activities Association, *1993-94 Official Handbook.*

Nathan, Joe. "TV School Coverage Sends Wrong Message." *St. Paul (Minnesota) Pioneer Press,* 6 September 1993.

National Collegiate Athletic Association. *Division I Graduation-Rates Report.* Overland Park, Kans., 1993.

National Collegiate Athletic Association. *1993-94 NCAA Guide for the College-Bound Student-Athlete.* Overland Park, Kans., 1993.

National Collegiate Athletic Association. *Revenues and Expenses of Intercollegiate Athletics Programs.* Overland Park, Kans., October 1990.

O'Brien, Richard. "Scorecard." *Sports Illustrated,* 22 November 1993.

O'Connor, Tim. "Widespread Problem Takes Toll on Students' Lives and Society." *Kansas City Times,* 23 May 1988.

Rawlings III, Hunter R. "Why Did It Take So Long?" *Sports Illustrated,* 21 January 1991.

Reece, Chuck. "Jan Kemp." *Ms,* January 1987.

Restak, Richard M. *The Brain: The Last Frontier.* New York: Warner Books, 1979.

Roberts-Wilbur, Janice, and Michael Wilbur and Joseph R. Morris. "The Freshman Athlete's Transition: Athletic and Academic Stressors." *Academic Athletic Journal,* Spring 1987.

Sage, G.H. *Power and Ideology in American Sport: A Critical Perspective.* Champaign, Ill.: Human Kinetics, 1990.

"Serious Sports." *School Administrator,* August 1993.

Southwest Missouri State University Study Skills Report, 1989.

Steele, Michael R. *Knute Rockne, A Bio-Bibliography.* Westport, Conn.: Greenwood Press, 1983.

Tamarin, Shirley and Alfred. *Olympic Games in Ancient Greece.* New York: Harper & Row, 1976.

Taylor, Phil. "Courted and Convicted." *Sports Illustrated,* 26 July 1993.

Telander, Rick. "Frank Baker." *Sports Illustrated,* 15 November 1993.

Telander, Rick. *The Hundred Yard Lie.* New York: Simon & Schuster, 1989.

Twyman, Gib. "Geography Class Studies Team Travel." *Kansas City Star,* 24 September 1990.

Walter, Timothy L. "Predicting the Academic Success of College Athletes." *Research Quarterly for Exercise and Sport* 58, 1987.

Wolf, Alexander and Armen Keteyian. *Raw Recruits.* New York: Pocket Books, 1990.

Women's Sports Foundation. *Minorities in Sports.* Northeastern University, August 1989.

Wulf, Steve. "Scorecard." *Sports Illustrated,* 21 January 1991.

Zirkel, Perry A. "Courts and Sports." *Phi Delta Kappan,* October 1993.

INDEX

ACKNOWLEDGMENTS

Photographs are reproduced with the permission of: p. 2, Swarthmore College Sports Information Office; pp. 6, 26, 33, 73, The University of Oklahoma; p. 8, University of Kansas; pp. 9, 20, Independent Picture Service; pp. 10-11, Auburn University; p. 12, Rutgers University; pp. 13, 14, 31, The University of Notre Dame; pp. 16, 83, John Ferko/Swarthmore College; pp. 18, 59, 72, 74, © Mickey Pfleger; p. 22, Mississippi State University; pp. 23, 30, 76, 77, 78, Macalester College; p. 25, Gerry Vuchetich/University of Minnesota Women's Athletics; p. 27, Harry Edwards; pp. 28, 63, The University of Nebraska, Lincoln; pp. 29, 67, © Manny Rubio; p. 34, Kevin Ross; p. 37, Texas A&M University; p. 43, SportsChrome East/West, Mike Kullen; p. 47, Jim Rousseau; p. 48, SportsChrome East/West, Robert Tringali Jr.; pp. 50, 51, 80, SportsChrome East/West, Brian Drake; p. 52, © 1993 Bruce Kluckhohn; p. 54, The University of Chicago Sports Information Office; p. 57, Fergus Falls Community College; p. 58, Scott Bauer, ARS-USDA Information Staff; p. 60, Lisa Hall/The University of Oklahoma; pp. 64, 95, © Lucille Sukalo; p. 71, Pasadena Tournament of Roses Archive; p. 75, Colleen Sexton; p. 81, Wendell Vandersluis/University of Minnesota; p. 84, The University of Minnesota; p. 85, J.D. Levine/Northeastern University.

Cover photograph by Andy King at Macalester College, St. Paul, Minnesota.
All charts by Laura Westlund.

About the Author

Gary Funk is an associate professor of education at Southwest Missouri State University in Springfield, Missouri. He is also the director of the Greenwood Laboratory School and the Center for Outstanding Schools. He enjoys tennis, cycling, hiking, and spending time with his wife and two children.